CHANGE
FRIENDLY FAITH SHARING
The Book

Tina Trent

ISBN 979-8-88851-135-0 (Paperback)
ISBN 979-8-89112-974-0 (Hardcover)
ISBN 979-8-88851-136-7 (Digital)

Copyright © 2024 Tina Trent
All rights reserved
First Edition

All rights reserved. No part of this publication may be reproduced, distributed, or transmitted in any form or by any means, including photocopying, recording, or other electronic or mechanical methods without the prior written permission of the publisher. For permission requests, solicit the publisher via the address below.

Covenant Books
11661 Hwy 707
Murrells Inlet, SC 29576
www.covenantbooks.com

To my husband, Tim, who is the greatest gift in this life that God has given me and has helped me be all God has called me to be. I love you. To Corey, Jason, and Steven. You have taught me the true love of God. I am thankful for each of you and love you with all my heart.

CONTENTS

Introduction vii
   Change 1 vii
   Change 2 x
   Change 3 xi

Chapter 1: Becoming a Friend of God 1
Chapter 2: The Good News 8
Chapter 3: The Bad News 12
Chapter 4: God and Jesus Are One 17
Chapter 5: Believing in Faith and Prayer 22
Chapter 6: Growing in God 31
Chapter 7: Ongoing Change 40
Chapter 8: First Things First 42
Chapter 9: Loving Others 50
Chapter 10: Fear versus Faith 54
Chapter 11: Sharing Your Story with Power 62
   Sample No. 1 Testimony—Childhood 70
   Sample No. 2 Testimony: I Am Glad to Know
      (Christian at a Young Age) 72
   Sample No. 3 Testimony—Adulthood:
      Before and After 73
   Personal Story Worksheet: Adult (Before and After)...76
   Personal Story Worksheet: Childhood 77
Chapter 12: Learning the Gospel Outline 79

A Practice Outline to Memorize	82
The Complete Outline	83
Scriptures	85
Stories	87
Chapter 13: Handling Objections	91
Chapter 14: Final Thoughts	97
Acknowledgments	99

INTRODUCTION

At some point in our lives, we are all looking for some kind of change. Some of the questions we ask ourselves are as follows: Can you really change? Can you really have a different life? Can you really be a new person or hit the reset button? Can old things be put in the past and all things become new? Is this all there is in life, or is there more? The answer is yes. The one who created you, God, says yes, and it begins with a personal relationship with Him. Can you have a personal relationship with God? Can you know for sure? These were some of the questions I had. This book is designed to help answer these questions and start you on the road to a changed life. It is in the power of the gospel, *the good news*, where we find the power to change us. When we have a greater understanding of the gospel, we are empowered to grow which results in a further changed life. The sharing of the gospel will keep us ever changing. Join me as we embark on a changed life, the good news of the gospel.

Change 1

I was born to a couple who seemed to have problems from the start. When I was nine months old, my parents were separated, and they got divorced when I was two. I rarely saw my father for visits. My mother was a wonderful, hardworking single parent providing for her only child as best as she could. My father's mother paid to send me to a private Christian school where I had to attend chapel/church services every day and wear a uniform. Our chapel services were boring and ritualistic, but many times in my upbringing it would be a place I would attempt to have conversations with God. He was kind of like an invisible friend, and I hoped He was someone who listened to me when I talked with Him.

My grandmother (my father's mother) loved me very much and was a very loving spiritual woman. She passed away when I was seven years old, which left me with no spiritual influence in my life but my private Christian school. My mother was raised in a different denomination but never attended church. She would take me to church on some Sundays and drop me off to attend a service.

By the age of twelve, I was a latchkey kid trying to figure out life on my own in many ways. Miserable at this time in my life, I told my mother, "If I have to wear that plaid uniform skirt or go to that school one more day, I'm going to hurt someone." She agreed by middle school to let me go to public school.

This was a chance for a new start in life, I thought, with a new image and new friends. I became popular quickly with many friends. I learned how to be accepted by fitting in, and many times that included partying and some not-so-good or safe behaviors—you can fill in the blanks. I learned how to be the life of the party, and still, there was a loneliness and emptiness deep inside of me at the end of the day. I began to make goals and dreams for my life that I knew would have to fill this emptiness and make me happy. I thought if I just graduated from school, which seemed so hard and full of drama, and get on to my adult life, then I would be happy. I set out to do that as fast as I could with all the bells and whistles. I quickly found out that cars, jewelry, money, homes, and relationships did not fulfill me either. Instead, I was left with a big gaping hole full of more baggage and consequences. I began to wonder what this life was all about anyway and why bother.

    I was in a very low, dark place in my life when a friend asked me about my relationship with God. I replied I was of a certain denomination where I had gone to school and church as a child. She then began to ask me if I knew if I was going to heaven when I died and if I was a friend of God. My first response was yes because I was of that denomination. But then I began to think about it. I really didn't know for sure!

    I began to ask myself: Can anyone really know for sure? Don't you just go through life doing the best you can with the cards you've been dealt? I was hoping that on the day I stand before God, the scales will tip in my favor. Or possibly, there was another way? The bottom line was I wasn't really sure. She began to share with me about God and His love for me and life eternal. She shared things with me I had never heard before! She went on to pray for me, and that day, my life changed. It has been changing ever since I became a friend of God, His child, and received eternal life. Something supernatural happened in that moment. It was like being wrapped in a blanket of love, peace, safety, and security like I had never felt before. Somehow, I sensed and knew there was a God. He loved me, and I was going to be okay. I felt for the first time that this life had meaning and a purpose for me.

At that time, I also felt two very strong emotions. The first was joy; this gaping hole in my heart was now filled with an inner joy and peace I had never felt before. I felt completely loved. The second was great anger. I thought to myself, *I went to a Christian school and church all my life. I even knew people that said they were Christians, and no one shared with me this incredible life-changing news!* I couldn't believe it! What if they had? Would my life be different? Would I have escaped some of the hurts and scars that I had already experienced in this life?

I prayed that day and said, "God, if You teach me, I will never let anyone come across my path and not share this good news. This is not just good news but the greatest news they will ever hear!" God heard me that day, and my life has never been the same.

Change 2

I started regularly attending a church and began volunteering. I began growing, learning, and understanding God more. This gave me assurance and confidence in my relationship with God and my faith. I attended training classes and went to an international ministry to be trained further to know not only my faith better but how to share the gospel effectively and train others. (This was an answer to my first prayer.) Anyone who knew me before this time in my life was saying, "What?" What a change. I now had peace, felt loved, and loved others like never before. I experienced a true transformation from the old me.

Change 3

Forty years later, I have not stopped sharing that good news called the gospel. I began sharing and teaching others—from pastors, preschoolers, and prisoners to kids, youth, and adults. I have shared and taught across denominations, in other countries, and in different languages.

There has not been a day that goes by—and even as I write this—that I am not amazed at how God has allowed me to share His life-giving and life-changing word with others. And you will be amazed as you share the gospel with others. They have an opportunity to change, and you are changed as well when you share the good news of the gospel.

One thing I firmly believe is that, that day in my life was not an accident. Nor do I believe it is an accident you are reading this book. What I discovered were some very powerful simple truths that *changed* my life forever, and I am confident they will change yours. The following scripture references come from the Bible. Let the journey begin.

The gospel is the *good news that heaven or eternal life is a free gift*; the gift of God is eternal life (Romans 6:23).

> For God so loved the world that He *gave* His one and only Son that whoever believes in Him shall not perish but have eternal life. (John 3:16)

However, there is the not-so-good news I call the *bad news*, and it's something called sin. It separates us from God because He is holy. What is sin? A bad thought, word, deed, action, or attitude. It is something we should have done but didn't, or something we did that we shouldn't. I would have blown it by 8:00 a.m. with one of these sins, if not all! The better news is we have *all* sinned or missed it in these areas, every one of us.

> For all have sinned and fall short of the glory of God. (Romans 3:23)

When I heard this, I realized I was in the right club. I thought to myself, *what about God and Jesus?* First, *God is loving and fair because He cares about us.*

> This is real love. It is not that we loved God, but that he loved us and sent his Son as a sacrifice or payment for our sins. (1 John 4:10)

Jesus is God who came to this earth as a baby, was born of a virgin, grew as a man and lived a perfect life. Then He died on the cross for our sin in our place to fulfill God's plan. He is the visible expression of the invisible God (Colossians 1:15).

All we need to do is believe by faith with all our heart. That's where it all starts.

CHANGE

> Believe in the Lord Jesus and you will be saved. (Acts 16:31)

> If you confess with your mouth Jesus is Lord and believe in your heart God raised Him from the dead, you will be saved. (Romans 10:9)

It's that simple. I believe the question God is asking you today is the same one He asked me. Would you like to receive eternal life and know you are God's friend and child? If so, say this prayer with me:

> God, I believe You created me, and You sent Jesus, Your son, born of a virgin, to this world to die for me, in my place, that I may be with You forever. Jesus, I ask You to forgive me of my sins and be my Savior and my Lord. I receive Your free gift of eternal life right now. In Jesus's name, amen.

If you prayed that prayer, you are a child of God and His friend forever. Sign and date this book so you will never forget this day.

Name: _____

Date: _____

CHANGE

This is one of the most assuring promises God says to us:

> I give them eternal life, and they shall NEVER perish; no one will snatch them out of my hand! (John 10:28)

I don't believe in accidents anymore. My life has been on purpose from the day I prayed this prayer. It is one incredible story that is still going on. I used to think living an exciting life was living randomly, dangerously without purpose, and with possible life-altering consequences. Now I know that living an exciting life is living on the edge with God. He has taken me to some amazing places I could have never taken myself—the exciting life of faith. Get ready for the journey. It's wild!

I truly believe the fact that you are reading this book is by God's divine plan. If you prayed the prayer, let me be the first to say, "Welcome to God's family!"

Change 2

The power to grow in God comes through being confident and having assurance in the gospel and that you are loved by God. And knowing that you are His friend and child forever, and nothing could ever change that. If you have already prayed to receive eternal life before today but sometimes question if you are really a friend of God, this is common. If you're not 100% sure, or you feel like you have made too many mistakes, these are typical concerns that come from a lack of assurance and confidence in the gospel. I want to encourage you to pray the prayer above as affirmation of your faith. Sometimes, we just need a reminder of God's promise or a reassuring new starting point. I pray you will never question your relationship with God again. God promises,

> Therefore, if anyone is in Christ, he is a new creation. The old things are passed away, the new has come. (2 Corinthians 5:17)

This book was written to give you clarity and confidence in your faith so that you may go on to grow in your faith and God's plan for your life.

Change 3

The third reason this book was written was for believers in Christ, Christians, which you are if you prayed today or any other time in your life. God and Jesus both said in the Bible to be fruitful and multiply and go and tell others. But if you just don't know what to say to others about your faith, this book is a tool that will help you learn a simple and clear way to share the good news of the gospel. It can also be used as a teaching guide to help you teach others to know this life-giving and life-changing good news. This book is by no means a full explanation of God, Jesus, and the Christian faith. It is intended to be a simple, clear way of the gospel so that a person can put their faith and trust in

Jesus and begin a relationship with God. There is nothing more fulfilling for a Christian than praying with a person to receive eternal life. You will sense a feeling of God's good pleasure (That is an overwhelmingly good feeling inside—like nothing else, a real joy). Be careful, it is addicting! My prayer is that you are getting ready to embark on a life-fulfilling adventure of a *changed* life. In the following chapters, we will break down each point of the gospel with more explanation, scriptures, and illustrations that will give you more clarity and further understanding.

Please know that I am praying for you, and specifically, for your growth in God. Also, I am praying for you to become His partner in His plan to go in to all the world and share the gospel. This is called the great commission. Now that you know, you can go!

> He said to them, "Go into all the world and preach the gospel to all creation. (Mark 16:15)

CHAPTER 1

Becoming a Friend of God

The good news is also called the *gospel*. It tells about the birth, life, death, and resurrection of Jesus Christ.

Becoming a friend of God

How do we begin this friendship with God? The first and most important thing we can know in this life is that we are a friend of God. When we receive Jesus as our Lord and Savior, we become God's friend. It is so important to know what you believe and to have confidence in this new friendship with God. We need to know that God loves us with everlasting love. What does that mean?

God loves you and me so much! He created us in His image and gave everything for Him to have a relationship with you and me for all of eternity. It's been said it will take all of eternity with God for God to show us how much He loves us. He wants you to know that and to be confident in His love.

> These things were written that you might KNOW you have eternal life. (1 John 5:13)

God does not want you to worry about or question His love for you. This is one of the main points of the Bible. He is not only our Creator but our father, and He loves us. If you have children or you had loving parents, you may begin to understand this kind of love. I have often said my children can make me sad or even really mad, but nothing could stop me from loving them. Why? Because they are my children. If I am human and feel that way, how much more does the God of all the universe love His children? He is our Father and Creator, who is love and has infinite love, who loves us with an everlasting love. His definition is as follows: God is love (1 John 4:8). This kind of love is called agape. Agape is the highest kind of love. It means an eternal love between God and mankind, and mankind for God—a self-willing, selfless, self-sacrificial, and unconditional love. We could preach a sermon on this one topic, but for now, let's keep it simple. There are many different definitions or uses for the word *love*: a friendship kind of love, family love, husband-and-wife kind of love, and self-love. However, the kind of love we are talking about here is agape. Not like "I love chocolate ice cream today and maybe vanilla tomorrow." This is the kind of love in which God gave His only Son to die in our place so He could offer us eternal life with Him.

In the Old Testament in the Bible, Genesis 15:6, we read about the friendship between Abraham and God.

> Abraham believed God…and he was
> called the friend of God. (James 2:23–24)

You can know today you are a friend of God by believing and putting your trust in Him. God wants you to have the confidence and peace that you belong to Him. No good parent wants their child to always be wondering if they are okay with their parents or question if their parents love them. Good parents provide a home and food for their children. Neither does God. How stressful would your life be if you had to constantly question these kinds of things? Yet 95 percent of the world wonders what happens when we die. Have I done enough? Am I good enough? And many more questions. That is the reason for this book; you can settle the big question once and for all and have peace. The peace that says "I am a friend of God, and the worst this life will ever get for me is that I will leave one day and go spend all of eternity with a loving God in heaven. Heaven is a place where there *is* no more pain, sorrow, or tears, and I will see my loved ones again."

This confidence that God loves me and wants to spend eternity with me and that He is for me confirms that He is a purposeful God. He has a plan and purpose for me. God, the Creator of all things, who owns and controls all things, wants what is good for me. The God who died in my place is the same God who rose from the grave on the third day and is alive now. Nothing is impossible!

Maybe as you are reading this book right now, you are going through a very rough time. This is where you begin to trust someone bigger than yourself to fix the problem:

He is the only one who can, and His name is Jesus. Maybe you are already a believer in God and Jesus, but sometimes you are unsure about your faith or your future; reaffirming your faith in Jesus will give you confidence. If you are already a confident believer in Jesus, be assured there are people all around you who are not and need to know this kind of love and peace.

As a believer in Jesus and understanding God's love for all mankind, know that He wants us to love His people and share this incredible news with them: the good news of the gospel.

> God's greatest commandment is, "'Love the Lord your God with all your heart and with all your soul and with all your mind and with all your strength.' The second is this, 'Love your neighbor as yourself.' There is no greater commandment than these." (Mark 12:30–31)

What about the Ten Commandments and all the other *do's* and *don'ts* in the Bible. Amazingly they all fall between these two. So as long as we are loving God and loving our neighbor, we are good! The problem is we can't even do that without His help.

How do you love God? We begin by trusting in Him and in His son Jesus and inviting Him into our lives, surrendering and making Him and His ways our priority. This doesn't happen automatically; our love grows over time as we spend time with Him and get to know Him. As we talk with Him (what we call prayer), read His word (the Bible), and obey Him, we express our love for Him. If my friend loves chocolate ice cream and hates vanilla, I don't give them vanilla and say, "Whatever." I go out of my way to give them chocolate because I know it makes them happy, and that makes me happy. It is the same with God. As you spend more time with Him, you'll understand more of His likes and dislikes. We want to please Him from a thankful heart because He has given us eternal life, a friendship with Him, and forgiveness for our sins. We want to please Him. This is an ongoing process to love Him.

Prayer

What is prayer? *Prayer is simply talking to God.* Just like when you begin any new friendship, you spend time getting to know the person. You talk with your new friend about their interests, likes, and concerns. This is the same way we get to know God: no conversation, question, or concern is off-limits. The truth is He knows them anyway but is waiting on us to initiate and invite Him into the conversation. He is always ready to listen.

Prayer consists of talking and listening. Many times we only talk to God when we are in a crisis, like a 911 or emergency call. "Thanks for the help. I will call again in the next emergency." Or when we need or want something like kids do with parents. They only call when they need or want something. Emergencies, needs, and wants are all good things to pray for, and we should pray about them; God is always there and wants to help us like any good parent. But He also likes to just spend time with us or to hear us say we love Him. He loves it when we are thankful for Him, His beautiful creations, and more.

If you have asked Jesus in your life, you now have a part of Him living in you, the Holy Spirit of God. He will communicate with you. You may ask how. You may have a thought or a feeling that is not usually like something you would think or feel. You may have thoughts of peace, compassion, concern, or an idea. You may have encouraging, kind, or loving thoughts. You may feel bad about something you did or said and feel a need to ask forgiveness. Whatever your thoughts are, they will always confirm what the Bible says. The Bible tells us what God is like and who He is; that is why it is important to read it. Also, developing strong Christian friends to guide you is important too. Everything with God begins in prayer. Even Jesus prayed, so we should too. Start today. Maybe your prayers could go something like these.

- God, reveal Yourself to me.
- Help me understand You.
- Thank You, God, for this day, that I am alive and for this beautiful world we live in.
- Thank You for Your son, Jesus, who died for my sins and offered me eternal life.
- Thank You for forgiving me of my sins.
- Thank You for my future.
- Thank You that You are always with me and You promise to never leave me.

There is so much we can thank Him for. We can also ask for things we need or want. Even things we are anxious about like health issues or when we need direction in our life. We can ask Him to help others. He cares about our every need. So don't let another minute go by without beginning to pray.

Having a specific time and place every day is a great way to begin a habit, like having a daily date. But now you can pray anytime anywhere, and He hears you. Just pick up the prayer phone. He always answers. As you spend time in prayer, your relationship with God will grow. This is another big part of our changing process.

Scripture:

> Abraham believed God…and he was called the friend of God. (James 2:23–24)

Illustration: Friendships begin and grow because we spend time with one another. Prayer is just talking to God like we would a friend.

Prayer: Father, thank You for the gift of eternal life that You purchased for me by dying on the cross in my place. And thank you for offering me this free gift of eternal life. I receive it now. Jesus, I believe You are the Son of God, that You came to this earth, born of a virgin, and lived a perfect life, suffered, died, and was buried. You rose from the grave and offered me eternal life. You are alive now sitting at the right hand of God and praying for me. I believe it and receive it now. In Jesus's name, amen.

CHAPTER 2

The Good News

> BUT the GIFT of God is eternal life
> in Christ Jesus our Lord.
> —Romans 6:23

Heaven, or eternal life, is *free* because God wants *all* to be in heaven with Him, and none of us could afford it. God loves us with everlasting love. His greatest desire is to spend all of eternity with us and showering His love on us.

> Who wants all men to be saved and
> to come to a knowledge of the truth. (1
> Timothy 2:4 NIV)

The greatest gift in the world is to have the confidence that you are going to heaven and that you are God's child and friend, both now and forevermore. This is the main message of the Bible.

> But these are written that you may believe that Jesus is the Christ, the Son of God, and that by believing you may have life in His name. (John 20:31 NIV)

> These things I have written to you who believe in the name of the Son of God, that you may know that you have eternal life. (1 John 5:13 NKJV)

It is not only *good news*, it is the *greatest news* you could ever hear!

Most people don't know about this good news!

The world we live in is full of stress. It is full of many what-ifs and things that are uncontrollable. It is why many take drugs, drink, and do other numbing practices to cope with anxieties of life, death, and the hereafter. Many people fear the unknown. It has been said, 95% of people in the world do not know if they have eternal life with God or have a 100% certainty of their eternal life. God does not want us to be anxious or fear His love or the life hereafter; that is why He wants you to know for sure you are His and His forever.

> For God so loved the world that He gave His one and only Son, that whoever believes in Him shall not perish, but have eternal life. (John 3:16)

We can have no part in receiving this gift except to freely accept it. God loved us so much that He gave us His very best gift. Jesus died on the cross to pay for our sins and offer us the free gift of eternal life.

The most common objection regarding eternal life is that *it is a gift.*

We think, *Surely I must do something or give something?*

We are programmed from birth to be good and work hard for things like good grades and a paycheck. Many feel they must be good and work hard to earn eternal life as well. *This is not true!* It has already been paid for; it is a gift because God loves us.

> For it is by grace you have been saved through faith and THIS NOT FROM YOUR-SELVES; IT IS THE GIFT OF GOD, NOT BY WORKS, SO THAT NO ONE CAN BOAST. (Ephesians 2:8–9)

I love illustrations or stories; they really help me grasp the point God is trying to get across. He uses this a lot in the Bible to help us understand better and many times give us visuals of a concept. I will use them in this book to help bring clarity.

Illustration: Parents' present

Let's say, at Christmas, my parents give me a big present that cost a lot of money. I open the box, and a big smile comes on my face.

It is the very thing I want! I run to my room to get my money to give it to my parents to help pay for this awesome gift!

But it makes my parents sad when I offer to help pay because it no longer makes it a gift, but something I help pay for!

Like the present, God wants us to receive the free gift of eternal life. It is not something we pay for or something we earn. It is a gift from God because He loves us.

If I even pay a penny for this gift, it is no longer a gift; it is something I got a really good deal on.

For a gift to be genuine, it must be freely received.

Review

Scripture:

> For God so loved the world that He gave His one and only Son, that whoever believes in Him shall not perish, but have eternal life. (John 3:16)

> BUT the GIFT of God is eternal life in Christ Jesus our Lord. (Romans 6:23)

Illustration: Parents' present

Prayer: Father, thank You for the most incredible gift ever, the free gift of eternal life. I receive it now. In Jesus's name. And thank You that it is mine forever because of Your great love for me that You want to show me now and for all of eternity.

CHAPTER 3

The Bad News

The bad news is sin, and it separates us from Him.
The bad news, or I like to say the sad news, is called sin. Sin separates us from God because God is Holy.

> Look! Listen! God's arm is not amputated—he can still save. God's ears are not stopped up—he can still hear. There's nothing wrong with God; the wrong is in you. Your wrongheaded lives caused the split between you and God. Your sins got between you so that he doesn't hear. (Isaiah 59:2)

This is why someone had to take away our sins, and the only one who was qualified was Jesus who was perfect and had no sin. He stood in our place. Now we can have a restored relationship with God. God has a relationship with us for one reason; His son Jesus paid for our sins in our place. The payment for sin was satisfied by the only one who was qualified, Jesus.

So what is sin? Sin can be bad words, thoughts, actions, or attitudes. Anything we know that we shouldn't do or that displeases God. Many people think it is violating one of the Ten Commandments. And yes, though that is true, it goes far much deeper than that. It can be an attitude of heart even if we do what seems to be right.

A child may give another child a toy but, in their heart, they are mad about it and become mean or angry. They did the right thing, but in their heart, it was not right. That's a sin. The Bible says do not murder, but Jesus goes a little further and says if you even think about killing someone, it's murder. Ouch! I realized at that point in my life I was in trouble because it seems like many times I get in my car to drive, and another driver makes me angry, and the murder rate just went up in my heart.

> You're familiar with the command to the ancients, "Do not murder." I'm telling you that anyone who is so much as angry with a brother or sister is guilty of murder. (Matthew 5:21–22)

It can also be *not* doing something we know we should do like helping someone when we know they have a need, like doing an act of kindness or giving generously.

> Anyone then, who knows the good he ought to do and doesn't do it, sins. (James 4:17)

The question becomes can anyone be without sin? The answer is *no*!

> All have sinned and fall short of the glory of God. (Romans 3:23)

Everyone sins. No one is perfect. There was only one person who was perfect, and His name is Jesus. That is why we need a Savior! This was good news for me. I knew I was in the right club. Sinner, I knew that I qualified.

Sin brings death. First a spiritual death separation from God for all of eternity. When a person does a really bad act like murder or hurting an innocent person and more, it can actually bring physical death as well.

> For the wages of sin is death, BUT the gift of God is eternal life. (Romans 6:23 NKJV)

Jesus brings life.

> I am the way, the truth, and the life. No one comes to the Father except through me. (John 14:6)

Sin also binds, blinds, and traps us. Sometimes sin looks like the easier way but never is at the end. Sometimes sin feels good but only for a short time. When we do right, God sees and rewards us.

Even after we receive eternal life, we should always keep a clear and clean life before God through daily repentance; simply ask for forgiveness and turn away from sin. This could be a one-time sin or a habit we have developed. The key is to continue to repent and ask God for strength to change. Many times, I will suggest a person take a piece of paper and write down sins they can think of that they have committed and ask for forgiveness. Then write this scripture across the paper and crumple it up and throw it in the trash as a point of faith. Because that's what God does when we repent and ask for forgiveness.

> But if we confess our sins to Him, He
> is faithful and just to forgive and cleanse
> us from every wrong. (1 John 1:9 NLT)

Some of us may say, "Well, I am a good person," or we know a person we think is a good person. But what is good? The Bible says no one is good, not one (1 John 1:8–10 and Romans 3:12). Yikes! Because good is perfection, and none of us qualify. This illustration shows us that one drop of poison contaminates the whole.

Illustration: A drop of poison

Suppose I had a glass of water and a bottle of poison. Let's say the poison is like my sin. Sin could be stealing, lying, talking badly about someone, disobeying, and more. Sin is choosing to do something we know is wrong. What if for every sin I did, I put one drop of poison in the glass? Would you want to drink that water? Of course not! It would make you sick! You might even die. We all have sin in our lives. Sin is like poison.

Review

Scripture:

All have sinned and fall short of the glory of God. (Romans 3:23)

Illustration: A drop of poison

Prayer: Father, I ask You to forgive me of my sins _____ (be specific about what comes to mind) and even for the ones I am unaware of. Help me in the days ahead to obey You and do what's right in Your eyes. Thank You from this day forward; as I sin, Your Holy Spirit will show me, and I will be quick to repent and ask for forgiveness. You say in Your word if I confess my sins that You are faithful to forgive me. Thank You. In Jesus's name, amen.

CHAPTER 4

God and Jesus Are One

> In the beginning was the Word, and the Word
> was with God, and the Word was God. He was
> with God in the beginning...The Word became
> flesh and made His dwelling among us.
> —John 1:1–2, 14

All other religions are man searching for God. Christianity is God searching for man.

This is the main message that separates Christianity from all other religions: Jesus was God in human form.

There are many scriptures in the Bible that state this fact. I have always said the Bible is really a small book to hold the words to life. For example, in comparison to a set of law books. But for such a small book, when God repeats something, this tells me to listen closely. It must be important, just as my words were when I was raising my kids. If I repeated myself, it was important. It could even be a matter of life or death.

So who is God?

This is a big topic, and there are many names for God, and I would encourage you to take some time at some point to look them up and study them. But for now, let's keep it simple. He is the Almighty. He is our Creator and the Creator of the universe. He is the sustainer of life and eternal life. He is in control of the here and now and in the hereafter.

There are many misconceptions about what God is like. Let's talk about a few. Some see God as a policeman who is out there policing everyone and waiting for someone to break the law so he can fine or punish them. This shows a justice side of God only and not a loving one. Some see Him as a grandfather type who just gives you everything you want and turns His head away from wrong. This shows an extremely loving side of God but does not show His justiciable side.

The last is He is just like the Grinch who stole Christmas or Scrooge in the movie *A Christmas Carol*. If you see God with this type of interpretation, you may see Him as the Grinch or Scrooge. These characters were just trying to make others' lives miserable and unhappy. That's not God at all. The description of God is, "God is love" (1 John 4:8). Plain and simple.

For example, God is the judge. He pronounces us guilty and sentences us to death. Then He gets up from behind the judge's bench, walks around and pushes us aside, and says, "I myself will take the sentence of death for you." In this way, He satisfies His justice and love.

This was a problem for us. God is holy and just, and we are guilty of sin. But God made a way to satisfy and not compromise His justice. He loves us with an everlasting love…through His son, Jesus.

CHANGE

> This is real love. It is not that we loved God, but that he loved us and sent His son as a sacrifice to take away our sins. (1 John 4:10 NLT)

Jesus is God, who came to this earth as a baby, was born of a virgin, grew into a man, and died on the cross for our sins. He came to fulfill God's plan for us so we could be God's child and friend forever. Here is the mystery: God is three persons, but still one God. He is God the Father, God the Son, and God the Holy Spirit. Many times, I use this illustration. I am a wife. I am also a mom, and I am a minister. I have three different roles, but I am the same person.

God the Father created us in His image because He loves us. God the Son died to pay the penalty for our sins. God the Holy Spirit was sent after Jesus ascended into heaven to empower us to live a godly and changed life. He will also be with us now and through all eternity. What a love, this can only be the God kind of love.

Illustration: Hot-air balloon

Suppose I am looking up into the sky, and I see a hot-air balloon. I know it's full of air because the heat is making it rise. The air on the inside is like God whom you can't see but you know He's there because you see its effects. The outside of the balloon is like Jesus whom you can see. The balloon is like Jesus, who is God with skin on.

> Jesus is the visible expression of the invisible God. (Colossians 1:15)

Jesus came to earth, was born of a virgin, died on the cross for our sins, and rose from the grave. Many people saw Him while He was on this earth after the resurrection.

> But God raised Him from the dead on the third day and caused Him to be seen. (Acts 10:40)

Jesus was God's ultimate expression of love to us. While on this earth, Jesus lived His life as an example for us to follow. He prayed for people, showed compassion, shared about salvation, forgave, served, and helped people, and more.

> Most assuredly, I say to you, he who believes in Me, the works that I do he will do also; and greater works than these he will do, because I go to My Father. (John 14:12 NKJV)

Review

Scripture:

> Jesus is the visible expression of the invisible God. (Colossians 1:15)

CHANGE

Illustration: Hot-air balloon

Prayer: Father, thank You for being full of love and for loving me with everlasting love. Thank You that You came for me, sacrificed for me, and gave me eternal life forever with You.

CHAPTER 5

Believing in Faith and Prayer

I tell you the truth, he who believes has everlasting life.
—John 6:47 NIV

Believing in your heart is where it starts.

> Believe in the Lord Jesus, and you will be saved. (Acts 16:31 NIV)

What does the word *believe* mean? One definition is to accept something as true or have faith. Jesus wants us to trust Him alone for eternal life. That is where it begins.

Jesus is the only one who can save us because He is the only one who died on the cross and rose from the grave for us.

Trusting in Jesus for eternal life is just the beginning. The following illustration is a good example.

CHANGE

The rescue

Imagine that I am in a tall building. I'm on the tenth floor. Suddenly I begin to smell smoke. The fire alarm goes off, and the elevators no longer work. I run to the stairs, but all I can see are flames and smoke. I can't go that way. I run to the window. I look down. It's not safe for me to jump. I am too high. Then, like a miracle, I hear the sound of a fire truck. I look down and see a fireman. He has a net. He shouts, "Trust me. I'll save you!" *Just like the fireman in the story, Jesus is the only one who can save us.*

> Jesus answered, "I am the way and the truth and the life. No one comes to the Father except through me." (John 14:6)

> If you confess with your mouth that Jesus is Lord and believe in your heart that God raised him from the dead, you will be saved. (Romans 10:9)

> For it is with your heart that you believe and are justified, and it is with your mouth that you confess and are saved. (Romans 10:10)

Prayer for salvation

You may have heard of many types of prayers to receive eternal life or salvation. Maybe a pastor of a church says a prayer and asks you to repeat after him. Or possibly, he asks you to raise your hand or come to the front of the church to receive salvation. The methods are as unique as the minister or person making the invitation. The truth is all God is looking for is a willing, sincere, and open heart.

Jesus desires that we ask or invite Him into our hearts and lives.

> Look! I have been standing at the door, and I am constantly knocking. If anyone hears me calling Him and opens the door, I will come in and fellowship with him and he with Me. (Revelation 3:20)

True love is voluntarily given or received for it to be genuine true love. If it is forced on us, it is not true love. We call that abuse or manipulation. God gives us free will to choose Him. Many people don't know this. I have heard some people say if God loves all people, why doesn't He just send everyone to heaven? Because again that would not be a choice.

Here's a great example: if a man approached a girl and said, "I have a ring. Marry me now!" she would probably be offended. But if he said it like this, "I love you. Will you marry me?" There's a huge difference! God loves us too much to force us to love Him. He loves us so much He gives us a choice. Salvation and eternal life are available to all who receive.

There is a story in the Bible of when Jesus was hanging on the cross dying between two thieves. One of the thieves on the cross next to Him said, "Jesus, remember me when you come into your kingdom." Jesus replied to him, "*Today, you will be with me in paradise.*" That was the thief's way of saying, "I believe in you, and I want to be with you forever in heaven." Jesus said, "Done!" (Luke 23:39–43).

There have been times when I have asked people if they would like to pray and ask Jesus to come into their lives and repent and receive eternal life, and they have responded with, "I don't know." When I asked why, the answer would not be "I don't want it," it was "I don't know how to pray." I have found I must be ready to help lead others to Jesus in a simple prayer. It's like showing them how to pray. In reality, if you say yes in your heart to Him, He hears you, but when we confess something with our mouth, we seem to be more serious about it. The Bible says out of the abundance of our hearts, our mouth speaks. This also opens the door for others to see how easy prayer is.

Leading someone in a salvation prayer is like introducing them to a new friend.

Leading someone in prayer is like introducing them to a new friend. They can now communicate with their new friend by themselves.

Here are some prayer points:

Point 1. The question: I believe the question God may be asking you right now is, "Would you like to receive Jesus and eternal life?" If yes, I will lead us in prayer. Will you repeat after me and say this prayer out loud right now? We will be asking for forgiveness of our sins, inviting Jesus into our whole life, and then asking Him to lead our lives.

Let's pray.

Salvation prayer:

Dear Jesus, I ask You to forgive me of my sins, come into my heart, and be Lord of my life. In Jesus's name, amen.

It's that simple. The Bible says if you pray and ask Jesus to come into your heart, you will be saved, and you will become a friend of God forever.

> I give them eternal life, and they shall never perish; no one will snatch them out of my hand. (John 10:28 NIV)

> For I am convinced that neither death nor life, neither angels nor demons, neither the present nor the future, nor any powers, neither height nor depth, nor anything else in all creation, will be able to separate us from the love of God that is in Christ Jesus our Lord. (Romans 8:38–39)

Now that you are God's child, you not only belong to Him, but He is also your heavenly Father. He wants a relationship with all of us, and He wants to care for us daily now in this life as well as the life to come. Jesus also wants us to trust Him for the things we need every day.

> I have come that they may have life
> and have it to the full. (John 10:10)

Things we need in this life include help, peace, healing, wisdom, material things, etc.

What do you need right now? Pray and ask Jesus to meet this need.

> Do not fear, little flock, for it is your Father's good pleasure to give you the kingdom. (Luke 12:32 NKJV)

Another great example of how to pray is the guideline Jesus gave us in the most famous prayer, the Lord's Prayer. I love that Jesus cared enough about His disciples to take the time to teach them how to pray. That's right. You are not the only one who is not skilled at praying. Neither were Jesus's disciples. They had to learn and put it into practice. I love the fact that years ago, Jesus knew what we would need to pray for every day and what would be important things to pray for.

Let's take a quick glance at the Lord's Prayer. We see it in two places in the Bible: Matthew and Luke 1. It must be important! Let's take a look at Matthew:

> This, then, is how you should pray:
> *"Our Father in heaven, hallowed be your name."* (Matthew 6:9–13 NIV)

Example: Start your prayer with who you are talking to, your loving all-powerful Father, and where He lives—in heaven. He has a heavenly view. He sees and hears everything. We can begin our prayer time with thanksgiving and acknowledging who we are praying to. For example, our Creator, Savior, Provider, Healer, our loving Father, and Friend, etc.

*Your kingdom come, your will be done,
on earth as it is in heaven.*

Example: Praying His will for us our family, friends, city, nation, and work... I could go on. There is no more perfect prayer then asking for God's will in our situation. We can always be specific. As we learn more about God, we will learn more about His will.

Give us today our daily bread.

Example: Praying for our needs and asking Him to provide what we need daily for us and our family and friends. Again, we can be specific about our needs and even our desires.

*And forgive us our debts, as we have
forgiven our debtors.*

Example: God tells us to forgive. This is hard, especially when someone has hurt us deeply. But it is a command because God does not want us to be burdened with unforgiveness. It is a heavy burden to carry, always thinking about the person who has wronged us, or thinking about how to get revenge or retaliation. He wants us to give it to Him and let Him handle it. He has forgiven us for a lot, and we need to forgive others. Forgiveness is not saying what a person did to you was okay; it is just forgiving. It is not a feeling it is a decision. We say, "I forgive [name of the person] and give them to you." This is a process, and it is not always easy. We need to ask God to help us. We may have to pray for this over and over. And it may take some time.

And lead us not into temptation, deliver us from the evil one.

Example: Father, help me identify temptation and strengthen me to resist the temptation or the devil. Your word promises if I resist the devil, he will flee. Thank You that greater are You in me than the temptation of this world. Your power is made perfect in my weakness. Thank You that no weapon formed against me will prosper (James 4:7, 1 John 4:4, 2 Corinthians 12:9, Isaiah 54:17).

Review

Scripture:

> If you confess with your mouth that Jesus is Lord and believe in your heart that God raised him from the dead, you will be saved. (Romans 10:9)

Believe in the Lord Jesus, and you will be saved. (Acts 16:31 NIV)

Illustration: The rescue

Salvation prayer: Dear Jesus, I ask You to forgive me of my sins, come into my heart, and be Lord of my life. In Jesus's name, amen.

CHAPTER 6

Growing in God

> You must crave the pure spiritual milk so you can grow into the fullness of your salvation. Cry out for this nourishment as a baby cries for milk, now that you have had a taste of the Lord's kindness.
> —1 Peter 2:1–3

Now that we are God's friend, we need to grow in Him. This is a daily, lifelong process, and it begins the day you become His child. God wants you to be successful in your Christian life. The better we know Him, the more we will be like Him, and the better we can share Him with others.

Now to grow in God, this is the way: *Bible, church, ask and pray, and don't forget to share the way*!

Points to growing in God

Bible: The Bible is the most powerful book in this world. It is the only book that has been outlawed in some places around the world. In fact, right now, in some locations just across the ocean, it is against the law to own a copy. Some people would give everything they have for a copy or even a page. People are imprisoned because they possess a copy; some have even lost their lives over it. It has had more controversy than any other book in the world. It has been burned, banned, and outlawed, and yet it remains the number one bestseller. That alone should get our attention.

It is the only book wherein when you read it, it reads you. It is alive. No matter how many times you pick it up and read it, you will find out more and more. Its truths are endless. It has the power to change you. Just pick it up and try it. Why? Because it's God's word. God Himself is talking to you through human authors inspired by the Holy Spirit. When I talk with people, sometimes they say, "God doesn't speak to me." Then I ask them if they have read His word today. If so, then He is speaking. This is how we get to know Him better, and we find out what He likes and dislikes. If I fall in love with someone, I spend time with them, and I learn what they like and dislike because I want to please them. If I know they love chocolate ice cream and hate vanilla, I don't serve them vanilla. You wouldn't do that to someone you love.

Read the Bible every day; this is very important in your daily growth as a believer. The Bible has been compared to your new instruction manual for your new life. It's also considered by many to be a love letter from God. The Bible is divided into two parts: the Old and New Testaments. A great place to start is in the New Testament with the Gospel of John. This book talks about God and His love. It is a good idea to learn about the Bible and its authors and how to study it, but don't let that stop you from beginning to read it today. Right now! It is powerful and life-changing!

> In the beginning was the Word, and the Word was with God, and the Word was God. (John 1:1)

> All scripture is God-breathed and is useful for teaching, rebuking, correcting, and training in righteousness, so that the man of God may be thoroughly equipped for every good work. (2 Timothy 3:16–17)

> Your word is a lamp for my feet, a light on my path. (Psalm 119:105 NIV)

Note: you can download a Bible app on your phone or computer for quick access and let the fun begin.

Church: This is important. This is where we learn about God and His word from pastors or professionals. Some people spend most of their lives studying God and His word so they can help us learn quickly and more efficiently. This is where we learn more about God and become part of a family that helps each other along. I have said humorously, going to church is not God's ultimate torment to a late Saturday night. It is not supposed to be torture at all. It should be a place of enjoyment. Most churches used to meet only on Sundays early in the morning. However, that is not true today. Many churches meet at night or during the week. You can find one that fits almost any schedule these days. Find a church that helps you grow in your knowledge of the truth, where people will care for you and be there for you.

> I rejoiced with those who said to me, "Let us go to the house of the Lord." (Psalm 122:1)

> Let us not neglect our church meetings, as some people do, but encourage and warn each other, especially now that the day of His coming back again is drawing near. (Hebrews 10:25)

Note: Church is not perfect, nor is it full of perfect people. If it was a perfect place, as soon as we started attending, it wouldn't be perfect anymore! It is like family; everyone is in a different place in their lives and has different personalities, but we are family and should all be loving, encouraging, and helping one another. Unfortunately, this is not always the case. If you have been hurt or offended in church, forgive and move on. If the church you find is not loving or accepting, don't blame God. People are imperfect and should always be growing. Find one you can grow and be a part of. The church has been referred to like ice cream; not everyone likes vanilla; some like chocolate or strawberry. Just remember growing can sometimes be a little uncomfortable. We call these growing pains. This is necessary if we are going to grow.

CHANGE

You may just need to bring some different flavor into the game!

Ask: Now that you have received Jesus's sacrifice and become a friend of God, the third part of God the Holy Spirit comes to live with you. Jesus told us when He was leaving this world that He would not leave us alone. He would send the Holy Spirit to help us.

> He said, I will not leave you as orphans; I will come to you. Before long, the world will not see me anymore, but you will see me. Because I live, you also will live. (John 14:18–19)

His name is the Holy Spirit. His job is to be our helper or one who comes alongside to help us. He is described as our comforter, helper, guide and so much more!

Jesus said after He was resurrected,

> But I tell you the truth, it is to your advantage (better that I go away; for if I do not go away, the Helper (Comforter, Advocate, Intercessor—Counselor, Strengthener, Standby) will not come to you; but if I go, I will send Him (the Holy Spirit) to you [to be in close fellowship with you]. (John 16:7 AMP)

CHANGE

We are never ever alone; the Holy Spirit of God lives in us to help us. Ask the Holy Spirit every day for help and guidance so that you might live an abundant life.

> But the helper, the Holy Spirit, whom the Father will send in My name, He will teach you all things, and bring to your remembrance all things that I said to you. (John 14:26)

> But you will receive power when the Holy Spirit comes on you; and you will be my witnesses in Jerusalem, and in all Judea and Samaria, and to the ends of the earth. (Acts 1:7–8)

Pray: Prayer is simply talking to God like you would a friend. When should we pray? The Bible encourages us to pray morning, noon, and night, all day, every day. There is no specific time anytime is a good prayer time. The ultimate goal is to have an ongoing relationship with God in prayer. There are times of intense need and even emergency situations. There are seasons of hurt, sadness, grief, and pain. Then there are moments of celebration, gratitude, and great joy. At other times, we need to make decisions, we fear something in our lives, or we have questions. We can pray during any of these times. Our God loves it when we talk to Him. He promises to guide us. He always hears our prayers. He is the one who knows the answers and knows the end from the beginning. He is the one who can handle our situation better than we can. Praying allows you to get to know Him and love Him. It keeps you from being anxious in an otherwise anxious world. Won't you pray and talk to Him today?

> Do not be anxious about anything, but in everything, by prayer and petition, with thanksgiving, present your requests to God. And the peace of God, which transcends all understanding, will guard your hearts and your minds in Christ Jesus. (Philippians 4:6–7)

> Casting all your cares [all your anxieties, all your worries, and all your concerns, once and for all] on Him, for He cares about you [with deepest affection, and watches over you very carefully]. (1 Peter 5:7 AMP)

> Be joyful always, pray continually; give thanks in all circumstances, for this is God's will for you in Christ Jesus." (1 Thessalonians 5:16–18)

Share the way: Be prepared and willing to share your faith with others about the good news of the gospel. This is also the ultimate way of serving others. This was Jesus's first and last command to His followers. The first thing He said to His disciples when He called them to follow Him and the last thing He said to all believers before He left this earth. That includes you and me as well.

> And he said to them, "Follow me, and I will make you fishers of men." (Matthew 4:19 ESV)

> Freely you have received, freely give. (Matthew 10:8)

> Go into all the world and share my good news. (Mark 16:15)

Bible, church, ask, pray, and don't forget to *share the way*—these five ways to grow in our faith. These are as essential as our heartbeat, air, water, food, and sleep. If we are missing one of these means of growth or slack in one of them, it will show in our life and spiritual growth. Something will be off.

When I am not feeling just right, I can go down the checklist of these five things and ask God if something is off. Or I can ask myself, is He encouraging me to increase in one of these areas. If you are feeling a little off, maybe you are not doing one of these things. Or possibly, you have neglected one or even have stopped doing these five things. Pray God will show you, or maybe He is saying it's time for a little more. In the next chapters, we will cover some very practical ways of sharing your faith and why.

Review

Scripture:

You must crave the pure spiritual milk so you can grow into the fullness of your salvation. Cry out for this nourishment as a baby cries for milk, now that you have had a taste of the Lord's kindness. (1 Peter 2:1–3)

Statement: Now to grow in God, this is the way: *Bible, church, ask and pray, and don't forget to share the way*!

Prayer: Father, help me to learn and apply each of these important steps of spiritual growth in my life every day and always, that I may grow fully and completely in You. Holy Spirit, keep me in every one of these means of growth until I hear, "Well done, good and faithful servant." In Jesus's name, amen.

CHAPTER 7

Ongoing Change

The third kind of change is where we continue to change every day. How do we do this? Change is happening as we walk with God daily by loving, worshiping, and obeying Him. The Bible says going from glory to glory becoming more like Jesus is a continual process with great benefits and rewards. This is called sanctification. Sanctification means to be set apart for a special use or purpose.

It's like growing up and maturing or becoming more like Him. We become more like our parents. We look more like them. We act more like them. We understand, love, and respect them more as we mature. I understand this may not be the case if you did not have good parents. Unfortunately this happens, and this is why forgiveness is so important. Although my father was not involved in my life on a regular basis and had some bad behaviors, this provoked me to be even more like God, my heavenly Father.

When my earthly father would show up at different times in my life, he would bring me a gift. It was a kind of peace offering. It was for the wrong reasons and to relieve his guilt. However, as a child, I didn't understand his motives, and the gift would make me happy for a moment. He did teach me gifts can make you happy even if it was temporary. I love to give gifts today. It brings me so much joy to make others happy. I love to see people happy and let them know they are important and that I care about them, and I am thinking of them.

Despite my father's motives or guilt, God used Him in my life to teach me how wonderful gifts can be with the right intent. Guess who else likes to give gifts? God. He is the great gift-giver. The greatest gift He gave us was eternal life, so we would never have to die and be separated from Him but could spend all eternity with Him (John 3:16). That's the ultimate kind of gift giver. I want to be a part of that kind of gift giving, and He wants me to be. He allows us to partner with Him by sharing the good news of the gospel and offering this gift to others. "He invites us to join Him in the family business." There is nothing more important to God than loving us and spending all of eternity with us. He gave us Jesus and eternal life for this very purpose and offers it to us as a gift.

This is called the great commission.

> Therefore, go and make disciples of all nations, baptizing them in the name of the Father and of the Son and of the Holy Spirit, and teaching them to obey everything I have commanded you. And surely, I am with you always, to the very end of the age. (Matthew 28:19–20 NIV)

CHAPTER 8

First Things First

> Whoever has my commands and keeps
> them is the one who loves me.
> —John 14:21

When I first became a Christian, a believer in Christ, I wanted God to know how thankful I was for His gift of love, forgiveness, and eternal life. I knew I couldn't earn His favor in any way. It was a gift I didn't earn or deserve. How could I express my love and gratitude? It was by following Him and obeying His word. This showed I was serious and loved Him. *Okay,* I thought, *just obey Him and love Him. Easy, right?* Not exactly, and He knew it. That is why He sent the Holy Spirit to help us. He knew this would be a process, and this didn't bother Him at all. He knew what He was getting in me, and that was nothing short of a hot mess.

I had many bad habits and distorted ways of thinking about life and faith. I needed to learn God's ways, the author of life. There was no better instructor. He had actually left me a manual in the Bible. So I started reading it, something I had never done before. You see, I came to the practical conclusion that I was not doing so well at running my own life. In fact, I had made a mess. I began to think about trying it His way. So as I learned, I began to put it into practice, and amazingly, I began to feel peaceful, and things began to get a whole lot better in my life. I didn't say easy. I said better and then easier for sure. You can't buy peace, but that doesn't keep us from trying. Boy have I tried to buy a lot of peace. However, He is the only one I have found who can give it. With all my faults and shortcomings, He still loved me and wanted me, warts and all.

He loved me anyway and would help me change. This transformation came as I learned His word and obeyed it. So as I began praying, reading His word, and attempting to put it into practice, I found out some interesting things. And guess what? It worked. And just so you know, I still have a long way to go.

As I began learning about Him, His word, and His ways, I realized that the Bible is not that big of a book. In comparison, look at a set of law books a lawyer must read and learn. Most of you reading this book may be too young to know what encyclopedias are. They came before the Internet, so Google them. The last set of *Encyclopedia Britannica* contained thirty-two volumes and weighed 130 pounds. They were by no means complete. They were books that were similar to dictionaries but included more information. They were outdated often. Yet the Bible remains timeless and is still unfolding. I quickly learned if the Bible repeated something, it must be important. I know as a parent, if I repeated something to my kids, it was important information to them and me. In the case of the Bible, God's repeated word is always important and for our good. One of the first things I read was from the Old Testament in Genesis 1:8, "Be fruitful and multiply." In the New Testament, the first thing we see Jesus say to His disciples was, "'Follow Me, and I will make you fishers of men.' They immediately left their nets and followed Him" (Mark 1:17–18).

He was speaking to them in terms they understood because they were fishermen. He was saying, "You fish for a living so that people can eat, but now you will fish for men so that they can have eternal life." He then went about sharing the gospel and showing His disciples how to do it. He did it in many ways: preaching, teaching, sharing stories, and hanging out with all kinds of people. He also prayed for people, healed the sick, shared meals with others, performed miracles, and so much more. Wherever He went and whatever He did, He pointed people to God, salvation, and eternal life. The greatest example in my option was the scene at the crucifixion where Jesus was dying on the cross (Luke 23:39–45).

Now I don't know about you, but I can only imagine if I had gone through the beatings and suffering that Jesus endured, I would not want to talk to anyone. I would be thinking about myself and wishing everyone would leave me alone. We see here that the most important thing to Jesus is His people—you and me. Even as He hung on the cross, He was still teaching His disciples what the most important thing to Him was…us!

After Jesus was brutally beaten, painfully crucified, and hung between two thieves, we see our greatest example. One thief mocked Him and said, "If you are the Son of God, save yourself and us." While the other thief said, "Jesus, remember me when You come into Your kingdom." Jesus said to him, "Surely today, you will be with Me in paradise." I must pause here and ask you, have you asked Him to forgive you and to remember you and take you to heaven? If not, stop now and tell Him. He will.

Here, we see Jesus between two people: one who wanted to go to heaven and be with God forever and one who did not. It was like He was telling His disciples, "This is what I want you to do. It is important to Me. You see Me doing it." Now in the words of Nike, "Just do it."

God said, in the beginning In Genesis 1:28 to be fruitful and multiply. We have seen Jesus call His disciples and say, "Follow me. I will make you be fishers of men." We have seen Him lead people throughout His thirty-three years of life on this earth and at His death on the cross with the two thieves. Now He died, and on the third day, He rose from the dead. He showed Himself to His disciples and was seen by over five hundred people before He rose to heaven (1 Corinthians 15:1–11).

Our last words are usually known as very important and what we would like people to remember that we said. Jesus's last command to His disciples and to us was to *go* and tell!

> Therefore, go and make disciples of
> all nations, baptizing them in the name of

> the Father and of the Son and of the Holy Spirit, and teaching them to obey everything I have commanded you. And surely, I am with you always, to the very end of the age. (Matthew 28:19–20)
>
> He said to them, "Go into all the world and preach the gospel to all creation." (Mark 16:15)
>
> Jesus also said: "You will be my witnesses." (Acts 1:8)

This was the great *commission*, not the great *suggestion*! You may be saying *what*? Not me. I can't do that! What would I say? What will people think of me? I would be scared to death. I know the questions because I thought about them myself. However, the command is real, and God did not leave you alone. That is one reason He sent the Holy Spirit to help us. God did not command it to torture us. Like everything with God, it was to bless us (make us happy and fulfilled); it also has great rewards. Just remember how you felt when the burden of sin and insecurity was heavy on you and how it feels now that it is lifted. It is like having the cure for cancer, but you are too afraid to tell anyone. That would be crazy. You have the cure to eternal death, and it is eternal life. Don't keep it to yourself. This is another reason for this book—to help you take the leap from believing to sharing. So, let's keep going.

Many people think it is the pastor's job to share the good news of the gospel.

> It is actually the responsibility of pastors to equip (prepare, train, and arm) God's people to do the work of the ministry (Ephesians 4:11).

Where do I start?

Prayer!

How do we accomplish anything in God? Through faithful, consistent prayer. This is where we begin. Prayer is talking to God and developing a relationship with Him. Through prayer, we get to know God and receive direction and boldness to do His will. He can turn our fear into faith. We also need to pray for others. Begin praying for others to come to know Jesus and receive eternal life. Ask another Christian friend to be in agreement with you in prayer about whoever it is you are praying for. Let the Bible be your guide. Pray the Word of God and His promises.

> That utterance may be given to me, that I may open my mouth boldly to make known the mystery of the gospel, for which I am an ambassador in chains; that in it I may speak boldly, as I ought to speak. (Ephesians 6:19–20)

Pray also that the Holy Spirit would

- *give you boldness,*
- *open others' hearts to receive from Him,*
- *provide divine appointments,*
- *give you favor with others,*
- *give you wisdom in what to say,*
- *replace fear with faith,*
- *do miracles for you,*
- *help you be His hands and feet here on earth.*

Find a need that a person may have, and if it is in your power help them, meet it without requiring anything in return. People don't care what you know until they know you care. This is kindness and love.

A prayer God answers: As you start your day, ask Him to send people across your path with whom you can share the gospel with. Make a list of people you want to see come to know Jesus. Take a minute now and write three names down and begin praying for them.

1. _____
2. _____
3. _____

Paul wrote to his disciple Timothy,

> I urge, then first of all, that requests, prayers, intercessions, and thanksgiving

be made for everyone…this is good and pleases God our Savior, who wants all men to be saved and to come to a knowledge of the truth. (1 Timothy 2:1–4)

Review

Scripture:

Therefore, go and make disciples of all nations, baptizing them in the name of the Father and of the Son and of the Holy Spirit, and teaching them to obey everything I have commanded you. And surely I am with you always, to the very end of the age. (Matthew 28:19–20)

Practical application: Write down the names of three people that you would like to share the gospel with. Then begin praying for them.

Prayer: Father, thank You for the greatest gift of all eternal life with You. Help me be obedient to Your greatest desire and command to Go into all the world and share the good news of You. In Jesus's name, amen.

CHAPTER 9

Loving Others

Love the Lord your God with all your heart and with all your soul and with all your mind and with all your strength. *The second is this: "Love your neighbor as yourself."* There is no commandment greater than these.
—Mark 12:30–31

Loving others is easy when they love us first. However, it is not always easy or automatic, neither is making friends. Many times we have to be intentional in befriending or loving other people. It starts with being kind and caring. It takes prayer, effort, time, sacrifice, and sometimes money. Our time is the most expensive thing we can give. It simply starts with seeing a person having a need and, if it is in your ability to help, meeting that need. This is what we call being the hands and feet of Jesus in this hard world we live in.

Pray and ask God to show you or make you aware of needs people may have and how you can help. Understandably, we can't physically help everyone, but at least we can always pray for them and ask God to help them. We live in a busy world, and we are all so busy. One of the most valuable things you have is your time. Many people just need someone to talk to or someone who will listen to them. You may not necessarily have answers, but you have the time to listen. Be sensitive to these needs around you, especially if someone has had a loss of some kind in their life.

When appropriate, ask questions; it shows you are sincerely interested in the person. We call these questions the *what, when, where, how,* and *whys*. This is a simple way to make people feel important and valuable, and let them know that you are really interested in them and genuinely care. Whatever you do, when they begin to answer or talk to you, don't look away, don't cut them off, or don't look at your watch. All of these actions communicate "I'm really not interested" without saying a word. These actions will speak louder than your words and can kill your kindness quickly. If they express a need, offer to pray for them. This is one of the most powerful things you can do for a person.

You have now just invited God into the situation, and there is nothing more powerful than that even if they are not believers. You can ask if they have faith or if they believe in the power of prayer. Even if they don't, many times they will allow you to pray for them. If they do allow you to pray for them, hold on. God loves to show off many times by answering these prayers. If you are comfortable with praying out loud with them, offer to do it right there and then! "Where two or more are gathered in my name, I am there" (Matthew 18:20).

If you are not comfortable with that yet, tell them you will be praying for them and then go home and do it! Don't just say it. Follow up with them and ask how things are going. Lastly a prayer I know God always answers is this. "God, send someone across my path today whom I can help." Make that your prayer every day and watch what God will do. Remember people don't care what you know until they know you care. Find a need and meet it. Pray for God to make you sensitive to those around you. Be kind and be a friend. Give an ear. Listen more and talk less. Ask questions. Offer to pray for them.

Beginning to develop a friendship with this person could take five minutes or five years depending on their openness to spiritual matters. Don't ever give up. Remember people are always moving from being closed to open about spiritual matters. You can ask them about their spiritual background. For example, "Did you grow up going to church?" "Do you attend church now?" "Where do you go and how often?" All these questions will help you determine where a person is on their spiritual journey and possibly help them. Never speak negatively about another denomination or get preachy; this can be very offensive and cause a person to back off. After you ask these questions, this would be another good time to show you are sincere, and be vulnerable and share your story. This helps earns you the right to share the gospel.

Lastly, don't forget to forgive. One of the greatest acts of love we can show is forgiveness. As Jesus forgave us, we need to forgive others.

Remember, "Be kind and caring and don't forget the sharing."

Review

Scripture:

> Love the Lord your God with all your heart and with all your soul and with all your mind and with all your strength. The second is this: *"Love your neighbor as yourself."* There is no commandment greater than these. (Mark 12:30–31)

Practical application: Pray for your neighbor, find a need, and meet it. Give them some of your time, forgive them, and ask sincere questions.

Prayer: Father, thank You for showing me how and helping me love my neighbor as myself. Give me Your heart and love for them. In Jesus's name.

CHAPTER 10

Fear versus Faith

> For God has not given us a spirit of fear, but of power and of love and of a sound mind.
> —2 Timothy 1:7

Years ago, when I first began taking my newfound faith seriously and God's word and applying it to my life, I was met with mostly positive responses from family and friends. Did I say *mostly*? Some were not because I began changing some of my usual behaviors with friends and family. I learned that some of my behaviors were not pleasing to God. This was my new desire and goal. I also learned that these behaviors were not good for me either. They did not give me the desired results I was looking for—a changed life. I will be honest I lost a few friends at first, but literally, every single one of them came to me later (in some cases, years later) and asked me about my faith. They had seen a change in me. Sometimes, they would even ask me to pray for them. God replaced each of these friends with new and better ones who became like family.

Still the thought of telling others about my faith and not being sure how to do it effectively frightened me terribly. No one wakes up in the morning and says, "Oh, I wonder how I can be rejected today." That's what I imagined would happen if I shared my faith with others. I thought to myself, *I've had enough rejection in my life.* I imagined that I would look like a religious freak! Like one of those pushy people. These were the very types of people I had walked away from rudely in my past.

Let me say here I am not judging anyone who feels they are supposed to do any of these things. That is between them and God, but for me, it was not appealing. This actually pushed me further away. Over the years, others have told me they felt the same way. However, I was determined to trust God and His word. My thought would be, *He was either God or not, so if I did what He commanded, it would be good. I knew it wouldn't necessarily be easy, but it would be good.*

As I learned how to share my faith clearly, effectively, and confidently, it became easier and more rewarding. Jesus trained His disciples He didn't just throw them out there and say, "Good luck." He said, "Come. Follow me, and I will make you fishers of men." However, back to my fear. The truth is I started praying and praying a lot. That was all I could do at first. I prayed for God to give me boldness and opportunities and to teach me how to share my faith. Then I stepped out. *Are you ready?*

In my first attempts, I would pray, go into a ladies' restroom stall, lock the door, and place a piece of paper on the back of the toilet that shared a gospel message with a prayer. I would listen to make sure no one was in the restroom, open the door, and *run away*. Then I would pray that God would send a person into that restroom to find it and receive eternal life. Don't laugh. It was truly what I did in the beginning, because of fear. But I was determined to do something more than praying.

I then enrolled in a class that taught believers how to share their faith effectively like this book. This class changed me first and then equipped me to help train others. That is the reason for this book and the ministry of *Friendly Faith Sharing*. Over the past thirty-five years, by the grace of God, I have had the privilege to lead and train thousands of kids, youth, adults, pastors, and inmates locally and around the world into a relationship with Jesus and help them to train others. Again, after I was trained and put what I learned into practice, it became much easier, fun, and exciting.

Why do we fear sharing the gospel?

The number one reason is we don't want to be rejected. Proverbs 29:25 states, "The fear of man brings a snare, but whoever trusts in the Lord shall be safe."

We fear the unknown. When we have never done something before, or we feel unequipped to do something, we become fearful.

2 Timothy 2:15 encourages us to "Study to show thyself approved to God, a worker who does not need to be ashamed, rightly dividing the word of truth." Knowing how to share your story and knowing the gospel will help relieve this fear.

CHANGE

Other reasons for not sharing our faith

You may be unsure of your own spiritual condition. If this is you, go back and read the previous chapters and pray the prayer of salvation. This is where it all begins.

Personal sin. Many times in our lives, we feel like a mess, and we may be battling a sin or two. I have some good news for you—we all are! Don't let this stop you; we are all a work in progress. The reality is the very thing you are struggling with could help someone else and keep you accountable or motivate you to do better. The devil would love to keep you from sharing the gospel by keeping you feeling not worthy, ashamed, or embarrassed of what people will think about you. You may be surprised. They may think a lot more of you than you realize and actually be grateful for you. Possibly for the rest of their lives and beyond.

This is a big one—condemnation. Don't be condemned. Another source of fear is condemnation (a feeling of not being fit for use). As Christians, God is changing us daily. We *all* have blown it! Often, we think we can't share our faith with someone because we are not perfect, or we still have bad habits in which God is working out. Let me encourage you, not one of us is perfect, but if we repent and continue to try to overcome, God sees our hearts and is always ready to forgive and help us.

The Bible says that a righteous man falls seven times and gets back up (Proverbs 24:16). God does not accuse us, only the devil. The Bible says he (the devil) is the accuser of the brethren (Revelation 12:10). It is his voice we hear when he says, "Don't witness. Your own life is a mess." On the contrary, the very thing we are struggling with may be what could help another person have hope and trust Jesus. Romans 8:1–2 reads,

> There is therefore now no condemnation to those who are in Christ Jesus, who do not walk according to the flesh, but according to the Spirit. For the law of the Spirit of life in Christ Jesus has made me free from the law of sin and death.

I do not know what to say. This is why reading this book or taking a class on how to share your faith is so important. Start with the chapter on sharing your story. Write it and share it with friends and family first. This is a great place to begin. We are called to be witnesses, not expert witnesses. For example, a witness says, "I saw or experienced something. I'm not really sure of all the facts, but this is what I saw and experienced." An expert witness gives you all the facts about the event through much studying and years of experience.

We are called to be witnesses—that was what happened to me personally and what I have come to understand and believe. An expert witness would be considered a pastor or Bible teacher; that is their field of study or profession. What you need to remember is it is just fine to say to a person who asks you a question that you don't know the answer to. In response, you can say, "That is a good question. *I don't know the answer to that.* But I will find it out and get back to you." Then do it. Look it up. I promise you will never forget the answer. Or you can call a more mature Christian or pastor. Then *make sure* you get back to them with the answer. They will probably appreciate you more because you were honest. Stay with them until all their questions are answered.

Note: Some questions are just smoke screens to hide their unreadiness. If you feel this, that's okay. Just back off and continue to love and pray for them where they are. Don't take it personally.

Always *remember* we do not have to try to pick green fruit (people who are not ready or ripe).

Many of us have had or know of someone who has had a bad experience while trying to share the gospel. In Matthew 9:37, Jesus said to His disciples,

> The harvest truly is plentiful, but the laborers are few. Therefore, pray to the Lord of the harvest to send out laborers into His harvest.

This tells us there are plenty of people out there who are ready. We do not have to try to pick green fruit! If a person is not ready. *Wait*, for it is not time. People are continually moving from crisis to calm in their lives. Pray that the Lord of the harvest would begin softening their hearts. Always leave them with kindness so they will be open to the next person God sends to them. Keep loving and accepting them. They may not be ready today. But one phone call could change that, and you are there or someone else could be. You could argue until they say okay. You may win the battle for them to get rid of you, but you will have lost the war. Many Christians think God needs defending; He is not offended; He is well able to defend Himself!

Lastly, have faith in God!

Fear and faith cannot operate together.

Begin where you are. If all you can do is pray for the people or ask them how they are today or if you can share your story, *do that*. As you continue praying and doing what you can do, *you will grow.*

Do you know? The greatest witnessing tool we have is *love*.

> For we walk by faith, not by sight. (2 Corinthians 5:7)

> Now faith is the substance of things hoped for, the evidence of things not seen. (Hebrews 11:1)

> But someone will say, "You have faith, and I have works. Show me your faith without your works, and I will show you my faith by my works." (James 2:18)

> You see then that a man is justified by works, and not by faith only. (James 2:24)

And now abide faith, hope, love, these three; but the greatest of these is love. (1 Corinthians 13:13)

Review

Scripture:

For God has not given us a spirit of fear, but of power and of love and of a sound mind. (2 Timothy 1:7)

Practical application: Do something bold to share your faith. Example: Offer to pray for someone. Ask someone about their faith. Tell someone your faith story.

Prayer: Father, help me share the good news about You and be faithful to Your command to go into all the world. Help me begin in my world and with the people you have placed in my life. Teach me. Give me boldness and opportunity. Holy Spirit, I receive You right now. Thank You for Your promise to give me the power to be a witness. In Jesus's name.

CHAPTER 11

Sharing Your Story with Power

> And they overcame him (Satan) by the blood of
> the Lamb and by the word of their testimony.
> —Revelation 12:11

Your story or testimony is one of the most powerful tools you possess as a Christian!

Every true Christian has a story of how God saved him or her. Your story may not be as dramatic as someone else's, and that is okay. But if you have trusted Christ as your Savior, you have one!

> That which we have seen and heard
> we proclaim also to you, so that you too
> may have fellowship with us; and indeed,
> our fellowship is with the Father and with
> His Son Jesus Christ. (1 John 1:3 ESV)

There are two vital parts of a story or testimony.

(1) Knowing what to say to every man.

> But in your hearts revere Christ as Lord. Always be prepared to give an answer to everyone who asks you to give the reason for the hope that you have. But do this with gentleness and respect. (1 Peter 3:15 NIV)

(2) Knowing how to say it to every man.

> Let your conversation be always full of grace, seasoned with salt, so that you may know how to answer everyone. (Colossians 4:6)

Let's take a quick look at the *apostle Paul's Testimony*. When Paul stood before King Agrippa in Acts 26, he spoke to him simply, logically, and clearly about his life before he became a friend of God and what his life was like after.

People can argue doctrine with you forever, but they cannot argue your personal experience. Your story or testimony opens the door to sharing the good news of the gospel. When we share our story with others, we are giving them a glimpse into our lives and our experience with Jesus without being preachy or pushy. Some people may respond to you when you begin talking about your faith with "that is personal." But when we share our story and a personal piece of our own life and spiritual experience with others in a language they can relate to and understand, they are much more likely to share with you.

Most Christians have never taken the time to write, practice, and share their story. They feel it should come out automatically. That is why most people don't share their stories. They don't feel prepared or confident enough, ready at a moment's notice. When you write, practice, and share your story you become more confident in sharing your story. This is crucial if you are serious about being an effective witness.

Without it you will miss many did I say many opportunities to share your faith and the gospel. So please, I can't express to you enough, don't skip this exercise. If you don't do anything else, take time and write your story. Yes, write it! I promise you it will change you before it changes anyone else, and it will change you every time you share it, even with another Christian. Sharing our story or testimony is a way of declaring our faith. It opens opportunities to speak with others. It builds up our faith and the faith of others. It is life-changing. Now let's get started!

You have a story to tell!
Why share your story?

- It says God is alive and active in the lives of people today.
- It's the easiest thing to share with people in the beginning because it is about you.

- Jesus called us the salt of the earth. Your salty story will make a non-Christian thirsty and hungry to want to know more.

There are many types of stories you can share and the longer you are a Christian, there will be even more! But to begin, we are going to focus on one, and it is for the purpose of sharing the gospel. Let's look at two options, adult or childhood. You probably have one or the other. Let me say here if you have had an experience of accepting Jesus as a child and then later rededicating your life to God, in most cases, it is easier to leave that out and pick up after you rededicated your life. Most non-Christians don't understand this. After a person becomes a Christian, this would be a good time to share about rededicating your life to Christ. This can bring encouragement to some as they hear you share. But for many, we do not need to share our rededication story, because it can be confusing to them at this point. However, we could possibly share it at a later time. Remember we need to talk in real practical, relevant terms that people can understand and relate to.

Another problem many Christians run into is that they use terms and lingo non-Christians don't understand or think is weird. Short, simple, and sweet works best!

The following are some simple guidelines and a worksheet to follow. First, pick one of the types you feel best relates to your story. Either the adult story or the childhood story.

Note: Concentrating on one story. Later you may write other stories about experiences you've had with God. After you write your story, read it and listen to it as if you were a non-Christian. Does it make sense or sound weird? If so, rewrite it until it is clear and simple.

Before we get started, let's pray: Father, help me be a witness for You. Help me write my story, learn it, and share it to declare You and Your faithfulness and goodness so others may come to know You and Your love. Let's get started!

>There are two types of personal stories
>Choose one type of story.
>Childhood or adult story.
>(Remember you can write more later)

Type 1: childhood

I am glad to know… this is how the childhood story begins. This type of story is for when you received Jesus at a young age or can't remember a time when you didn't have eternal life and were a friend of God. In this story, you will share why you are glad to know you have eternal life and are a friend of God. You may want to refer to the childhood samples 1 and 2 on the following pages.

Your story should be a short sample of something God has done in your life, with a short descriptive illustration. Not an autobiography! You will have plenty of time to share more as your friendship with the person grows.

A short salty story will make them thirsty to want to know more.

CHANGE

Consider what God has done for you during your life. Think about how He has met a need, brought you through a difficult experience, or answered a prayer.

A childhood story will tell about how God was there for you or how He was faithful in your life and gave you peace or gratitude.

Type 2: adult

An adult story will give a before and after version of your life. (See the samples and worksheets for help.) Choose one life concept. If you are like me you could talk about any of these examples. They are all applicable to my life, but for this assignment, choose only one.

Examples:

- *emptiness to purpose*
- *rejection to acceptance*
- *fear to peace*
- *depression to hope*
- *sickness to healing*

Now you are ready to begin! Choose your story type, choose one life experience, read over the following checklist, pray, and ask God to help you write your story! Note: Don't overthink. Then trust your first instinct and go!

Story
Checklist

- Use descriptive language to help people visualize what you are saying. For example, I felt like I had an empty hole in my life.
  I felt like I was always walking around with a heavy backpack on.
  I felt like I was living in a constant storm.
- Share examples from your own life.
- Keep it short; no more than one page or one to two minutes in length. (This is very important.)
- Practice sharing it with a Christian friend.
- Share that you received eternal life but not the specifics. Note: this experience will vary for each person. For example, if you say I went down front at church and prayed to become a friend of God. The person you are sharing with may think that is the only way they can become a friend of God and receive eternal life. For example, they may not realize they can receive eternal life sitting in a living room, in a car, or a coffee shop. So instead, you may want to just say, "And then I became a friend of God." Leaving the exact circumstances surrounding your acceptance of Christ out leaves it open for them and God to choose their experience. It may just be praying with you.
- Don't use a lot of Christian talk in your story. I like to call this Christianese. This includes terms

or phrases such as "washed in the blood," "blessed," or "praise the Lord." A nonbeliever may not understand what you are talking about, and to them it sounds weird, preachy, or possibly, even like a foreign language! (Remember what you thought before you became a believer.) Speak in relevant real terms.

- Keep the sides of good news/bad news of your story in balance. Not too much before or after.
- If *rededication* is part of your story, you have two choices. Omit that part or begin with it after you've rededicated your life. In most cases, a nonbeliever will not understand this or may never experience it. However, your rededication story can be very effective when used later to encourage new believers or someone who is in that place in their life.

The following are some sample testimonies:

Sample No. 1 Testimony—Childhood

I am glad to know (Christian at a young age)

I am glad to know I have eternal life, and I am a friend of God because it has been the foundation on which I have built my life through the greatest and hardest days. I was fortunate to be raised in a happy, stable, big family. We lived on the oceanfront, and my childhood memories were filled with bike riding, beach parties, cookouts, and so much fun. At ten years old, I watched my parents sell everything they had and moved all six of us into a two-bedroom condo during a recession. My father downsized his construction company and for three years worked to survive. Thankfully, things turned around and his business thrived once again.

When I was twenty-six years old, I got a phone call that my dad had a heart attack and that I needed to come to the hospital. I frantically drove to the hospital, and my brother ran over and grabbed me and would not let me see my father coming out of the ambulance. My brother knew he had died. When I arrived, the whole waiting room was already filled, and my vivid memory was that everyone was crying and staring at me with pity. A few minutes later, the doctor who was a close family friend knelt in front of my mother and told us the news. We already knew in our hearts that our beloved godly father was gone.

Those days, weeks, and months were the darkest days of my life. I felt I was lost in an ocean of grief. Thanks to God and close friends who prayed and loved me through this life transition, I saw God take care of my family. I knew God as my heavenly Father who cares for His children like our earthly dad cared for us.

Throughout my life as a wife, mother, and leader, my faith in God has been an anchor as I faced my own challenges. Because of what I experienced, I have been able to help many others who experienced a sudden loss. What I am most thankful for is that God had always provided for and sustained my family. *But the greatest thing is knowing that I have eternal life, and I am a friend of God*, and one day I will see my father again in heaven.

CHANGE

Sample No. 2 Testimony
I Am Glad to Know (Christian at a Young Age)

I am glad to know

I am a friend of God and have eternal life. From the time I was a young, I have had the confidence God was my friend. Through many challenges and storms of life, no matter how hard they got, or when I didn't always understand, at the end of the day, I had peace everything would be okay, and I was not alone.

One summer, my family and I were taking a trip to the mountains. It was a good day. We were all laughing and having fun. We were traveling down a very narrow road with drop-offs on each side. All of a sudden it began to rain, and the road became very slippery. The car began to slide back and forth. We all became quiet and serious. Then suddenly, my dad lost control of the car, and we began to spin like a top.

At that moment, fear gripped us, and I didn't know what would happen. It was like one of those moments where your life flashes before your eyes, and I thought we were going over the edge and we were all about to die. At that moment I prayed, and a peace filled me like it had so many times before. After a few seconds later, which seemed like an eternity, like a miracle, the car stopped spinning, and we were safely on the road. That was a terrifying moment for me and my family. I am glad we were all safe. *But the greatest thing I know is if something tragic would have happened, I have eternal life, and I am a friend of God.*

CHANGE

Sample No. 3 Testimony—Adulthood
Before and After

Before

When I was two, my parents divorced, and I was an only child raised by a single mom. I didn't have the consistent love of a father around and in my life. My grandparents sent me to private school where I had to go to the mandatory school chapel services every day until I was in middle school. But other than that, there was no church upbringing in my home.

When I became a teenager, I begged my mom to let me go to the public school where all my friends attended. She agreed, and as soon as I began going to that school, my world seemed to open up with endless opportunities. I became popular and had lots of friends, yet there was still a void in my life. Something was missing.

I set out to fill this void with friends, parties, relationships, and nothing seemed to work. The harder I seemed to search for it, the larger the void became. I thought if I can just get out of school, marry a bodybuilding husband, drive a black corvette, and have a big diamond ring, then I will be happy. Well, to my surprise I was working out in a gym, I met a guy who bench-pressed over five hundred pounds, drove a black corvette, and eventually gave me a two-carat diamond ring! It seemed as if all my dreams had come true, and this emptiness would finally be filled. Well, not only was the void not filled, it became even bigger. Tragically my marriage ended in divorce, and my life turned into a disaster. I thought if this was what life was all about, why bother, and I hit the lowest point of my life.

After

It was then that a friend shared with me about eternal life and my life changed. I found out the awesome God of the universe created me, loved me, and had a plan for my life that only I could fulfill. The void was filled. I had peace and joy that I had never had before. Shortly after that, I met my second husband who also drove a black sports car and gave me a beautiful diamond ring. We have been married for thirty-five years. We have three grown, successful children, and we live in a home that is nicer than we could have ever imagined. I have had the privilege of traveling the world and so much more. The things in my life have far surpassed my desires or imagination.

But the greatest thing is I know I have eternal life, and I am a friend of God.

Note: This testimony has a before and after. It is simple and short with descriptive language. It has told you a lot about the person in a short time. Notice that it starts and ends on the same topic—eternal life and friend of God. It does not use confusing terms that a non-Christian would need an explanation in order to understand. For example: *saved, born again, became a Christian, redeemed*. These are true terms but need an explanation to a nonbeliever.

In the above stories, we started and stopped on the same topic, eternal life and friendship of God, and did not use confusing terms. It is also good not to use a specific age, especially if you have a childhood story and are talking to an adult. They may think your story does not apply to them because they are an adult. This is solved by simply omitting your age.

Remember these testimonies have a purpose—to earn the right to share the gospel with a person without becoming too preachy and losing an opportunity to share the gospel. There are many kinds of testimonies. This format of sharing your story is specifically for helping a person receive eternal life. Once you master this, you will feel more comfortable applying it to different stories in your life. Trust the process. It is proven, and hundreds of thousands of people have received eternal life through using these tools. As you trust this process, you will see how the Holy Spirit will take over and tailor your story to each situation. Plan and prepare, and the Lord will direct your steps.

In the following pages are sample worksheets that you can use to help you write your story after you choose which type applies to you, adult conversion or childhood.

CHANGE

Personal Story Worksheet
Adult (Before and After)

Before I became a friend of God

_____
_____
_____
_____
_____
_____
_____
_____
_____
_____

Then I became a friend of God.
After I became a friend of God. (Choose *one* positive experience.)

_____
_____
_____
_____
_____
_____
_____
_____
_____
_____

The greatest thing is I know I have eternal life, and I am a friend of God.

Personal Story Worksheet
Childhood

I am glad to know I am a friend of God.

_____
_____
_____
_____
_____
_____
_____
_____
_____
_____
_____
_____
_____
_____
_____
_____
_____
_____
_____
_____

The greatest thing is I know I have eternal life, and I am a friend of God.

Congratulations! You have made it through two of the hardest parts. Getting started and writing your story. Just a reminder: we have a real enemy (Satan), and the last thing he wants you to do is to become effective at sharing your faith! Now congratulate yourself, and let's keep going.

It's been said that the devil has already lost you, and he cares nothing about your church attendance or busy church work. However, if he can stop you from sharing your faith and leading people to Christ, he has kept you from taking people from him, and he has won.

Review

Scripture:

And they overcame him (Satan) by the blood of the Lamb and by the word of their testimony. (Revelation 12:11)

Practical application: *Don't* skip this lesson. Write your story, and share it with someone. It is powerful, and it will change your life!

Prayer: God, thank You that You came after me because You loved me. I have a story to tell. Give me the boldness to open my mouth and share my story. I pray You would lead me to opportunities to share it because many need to hear it. In Jesus's name, amen.

CHAPTER 12

Learning the Gospel Outline

In the next few pages, we will look at the *Friendly Faith Sharing* outline when sharing the gospel. Now I know some of you could be saying, "I don't need to learn an outline. I can share about Jesus without it." I'm sure many of you can. Let me encourage you to take the time to learn it. If I had not been taught, I could have easily gone through most of my Christian life without leading a single person to Christ. But as I write this book today, I have had the privilege of leading thousands from all walks of life and around the world, and you can too!

This would be a good time to honestly ask yourself a few questions: When was the last time I shared my story or the gospel? Am I able to give a clear concise explanation of the gospel? Am I comfortable leading someone in a salvation prayer? Can I effectively share with them after their conversion, how to continue to grow in their faith? Am I confident in what I share? What if I am interrupted, can I successfully pick up where I left off? Can I help a new believer learn how to share their faith?

Let me say I know there are many great methods of sharing your faith out there, and if you are effectively using one that is great, maybe you will pick up some more good tips from this book. However, if you do not know how to effectively share your faith, take time to learn. Yes, learn! For most if not all of us, sharing the gospel does not come automatically to be effective. It takes training and practice. If it was the most important thing to Jesus, shouldn't it be to us?

The following is an outline you can learn and yes memorize. You can write it, type it, audio record it, and listen back to it. You can even use flash cards. Whatever helps you memorize. As you learn and memorize, you will go automatically through each point with confidence, and interruptions won't trip or shake you up. If you work on it faithfully and consistently, you can really get it. You can use it like a devotional for the next few weeks and ask God to help you and speak to you through it. You can ask a friend to join you, and the two of you can do it together to help one another and keep each other accountable.

You can teach *FFS* or this book in a Bible study by using the outline and prayers. Be creative but most of all just do it! We will start with a basic outline, and then we will add to it as we go along. We can begin with the five main points and then add statements, scriptures, and illustrations.

Five main points

Let's start with the five main points of the gospel by using something you have with you all the time, your hand. Memorize these five points.

1. The good news
2. The bad news
3. God and Jesus
4. Believing in faith and prayer
5. Growing in God

The hand

1. The good news—use your thumb in the pointing up motion of thumbs up for the good news.
2. The bad news—use your same thumb in the pointing down motion for the bad news.
3. God and Jesus—use the pointer and middle finger together in a motion pointing to heaven. God and Jesus are one.
4. Believing in faith and prayer—use the ring finger. It represents a commitment to Christ and is like a couple repeating their wedding vows to one another as a confirmation of their commitment this represents praying the salvation prayer.
5. Growing in God—use the pinky finger representing little faith in a big God.

There you go the five main points of the gospel!

Let's keep going.

A Practice Outline to Memorize

Why memorize?
Some feel memorizing an outline or having a plan to share the gospel is unspiritual and runs counter to faith. On the contrary, having a plan and memorizing the gospel outline is evidence of faith. Memorizing is very liberating; it frees us to be led by the Spirit of God to personalize the gospel to fit a person's needs. It also releases us from fear and anxiety when sharing the gospel. If you will take the time to learn the outline and be prepared, God will use you.

> Study to show thyself approved, a workman that needs not be ashamed. (2 Timothy 2:15)

Be a friend: Remember to take time to befriend people before sharing the gospel with them.

Be courteous and kind. Ask questions: What? Where? When? Why? Listen. Watch your body language and facial expressions. Make eye contact and smile. Be careful not to look away or interrupt them when they are talking. Remember, your everyday lifestyle speaks volumes.

Your story: Sharing your personal story or testimony creates a desire to hear the gospel, or a desire to hear more about God.

The gospel: Good news, bad news, God, Jesus, believe in faith and prayer, growing in God.

Scripture memorization: Scriptures bring the gospel to life, give us confidence, and help new believers with the Bible.

Stories: Stories help make the gospel relevant for today, give people a better understanding, and reinforce the gospel.

Memorization of the gospel outline will help make you an effective witness. It will cost you something, but the joy and rewards far outweigh the cost!

The Complete Outline

Check off the list.
____ Be a friend.
____ Share your story.

Good news—heaven is free.
____ Heaven or eternal life is a free gift. (Romans 6:23)
____ The gift of God is eternal life.
____ For God so loved the world that He gave His one and only Son that whoever believes in Him shall not perish but have eternal life. (John 3:16)
____ Parents' present

Bad news—is sin and it separates us from Him.
____ What is sin? A bad word, deed, action, or attitude.
____ For all have sinned and fallen short of the glory of God. (Romans 3:23)
____ The poison

God and Jesus are one.
___ God is loving and fair because He cares about us.
___ This is real love. It is not that we loved God, but that He loved us and sent His Son as a sacrifice to take away our sins. (1 John 4:10)
___ Jesus is God who came as a baby, grew as a man, and died on the cross to do God's plan.
___ Hot-air balloon
___ He is the visible expression of the invisible God. (Colossians 1:15)

Believe in faith—believe in your heart that's where you start.
___ Believe in the Lord Jesus and you will be saved. (Acts 16:31)
___The rescue
___ If you confess with your mouth Jesus is Lord and believe in your heart God raised Him from the dead, you will be saved. (Romans 10:9)
___ Would you like to pray and ask Him into your life today?
___ Repeat after me.

Suggested prayer: Dear Jesus, I ask You to forgive me of my sin. Come into my heart and be the Lord of my life. In Jesus's name, amen.

Grow in God—this is the way.
___ Bible. Read and study God's word every day. It's our instruction manual.

CHANGE

___ Church. Attend regularly with other believers. This is where we learn and cheer each other on.

___ Ask. The Holy Spirit to teach and helps us every day.

___ But the Helper, the Holy Spirit, whom the Father will send in My name, He will teach you all things, and bring to your remembrance all things that I said to you. (John 14:26)

___ Pray. Talk to God every day, like you talk to a friend.

___ Share the way. Tell others.

___ Jesus says Go into all the world and share my good news. (Mark 16:15)

___ Close in prayer. Ask if there is anything you can pray for them about.

Scriptures

Good news

....The gift of God is eternal life. (Romans 6:23)

For God so loved the world that He gave his one and only Son, that whoever believes in Him shall not perish but have eternal life. (John 3:16)

Bad news

For all have sinned and fall short of the glory of God. (Romans 3:23)

God and Jesus

> This is real love. It is not that we loved God, but that he loved us and sent his Son as a sacrifice to take away our sins. (1 John 4:10)

> He is the visible expression of the invisible God. (Colossians 1:15)

Believe in faith

> Believe in the Lord Jesus and you will be saved. (Acts 16:31)

> If you confess with your mouth Jesus is Lord and believe in your heart God raised Him from the dead, you will be saved. (Romans 10:9)

Ask (the Holy Spirit)

> But the Helper, the Holy Spirit, whom the Father will send in My name, He will teach you all things, and bring to your remembrance all things that I said to you. (John 14:26)

Share the Way

Jesus says, "Go into all the world and share my good news." (Mark 16:15)

Stories

Good news
Parents' present

Let's say, on Christmas, my parents gave me a big present that cost a lot of money. I'd open the box, and a big smile would come on my face. It is the very thing I want! I'd run to my room to get my money to give it to my parents to help pay for this awesome gift! But it would make my parents sad when I would offer to help pay because it no longer makes it a gift but something I help pay for!

Like the present, God wants us to receive the free gift of eternal life. It is not something we pay for, or something we earn. It is a gift from God because He loves us.

Bad news
A drop of poison

Suppose I had a glass of water and a bottle of poison. Let's say the poison is like my sin. Sin could be stealing, lying, talking badly about someone, disobeying, and more. Sin is choosing to do something we know is wrong. What if, for every sin I did, I put one drop of poison in the glass? Would you want to drink that water? Of course not! It would make you sick! You might even die. *We all have sin in our lives. Sin is like poison.*

God and Jesus
Hot-air balloon illustration

Suppose I am looking up into the sky, and I see a hot-air balloon. I know it's full of air because the heat is making it rise. The air on the inside is like God whom you can't see, but you know it's there because you can see its effects. The outside of the balloon is like Jesus whom you can see. *The balloon is like Jesus, who was God with skin on!*

Believing in faith
The rescue

Imagine that I am in a tall building. I'm on the tenth floor. Suddenly I begin to smell smoke. The fire alarm goes off, and the elevators no longer work. I run to the stairs, but all I can see are flames and smoke. I can't go that way, so I run to the window and look down. It's not safe for me to jump. I am too high. Then, like a miracle, I hear the sound of a fire truck. I look down and see a fireman. He has a net. He shouts, "Trust me. I'll save you!" *Just like the fireman in the story, Jesus is the only one who can save us.*

Note: When sharing the stories, it is important for them to make sense and tie it back to the main point, so even if you forget parts of the story or change it, just remember to tie it back to the point of the gospel. Make sure you memorize the last tie-in line.

CHANGE

The Friendly Faith Children's Rhyme is part of our Friendly Faith kid's curriculum. It also includes hand motions. Many adults and youth have expressed that the rhyme has helped them learn the gospel outline, so I have included it as an extra helping tool.

The Friendly Faith Children's Rhyme

The good news is heaven is free!
Would you like to go there with me?
The bad news is sin, and it keeps us from Him.
But God is loving and fair because He cares.

Jesus is God who came as a baby,
grew as a man, died on the cross,
to do God's plan.
All you have to do is
Believe in your heart,
that's where it starts.

Will you pray and ask Him into your life today?

Repeat after me:

"Dear Jesus, I ask You to forgive me of my sins,
come into my heart, and be Lord of my life.
In Jesus's name, amen."

Now, to grow in God, this is the way:
Bible, church, ask and pray, and don't
forget to share the way.

Review

Scripture:

>Study to show thyself approved, a workman that needs not be ashamed. (2 Timothy 2:15)

Practical application: Read, study, memorize, and practice with a friend.

Prayer: Jesus, Your last command was to go into all the world and preach the gospel. You have given us the mind of Christ and the Holy Spirit to remind us of all things. Help our minds as we study, and use us in a mighty way. In Jesus's name.

CHAPTER 13

Handling Objections

Biblical basis:

> Sanctify the Lord God in your hearts: and be ready always to be able to give an answer to every man that asks you a reason for the hope that is in you with meekness and fear (respect). (1 Peter 3:15)

Notice in this key passage, the apostle focuses on two basic conditions for handling objections:

- Be *ready* with your answer.
- Your *attitude* needs to be respectful.

Both are important because it's possible to give good answers with bad attitudes, and this weakens your witness.

Remember, your primary task is to *witness* (share the gospel).

- You are not a judge, jury, or defense attorney; you are a witness.
- Millions of people have trusted Christ without ever raising one difficult question.
- Don't expect everyone you meet to raise objections.

Realize when they do raise objections, many of those objections may be sincere questions.

- Until proven otherwise, assume every question is a sincere search for the truth: "Love believeth all things."
- Express appreciation: "Thank you for asking that question!"

Resist the tendency to argue.

- You never win when you argue.
- Too often we "win a battle and lose the war."
- Show a positive attitude by meeting every objection with, "I'm glad you said that!"

Recognize that some objections are smoke screens behind which people are hiding. Sometimes, it could be a bad habit or, possibly, something they feel guilty for.

- Sometimes it's fear or a device of the devil to blind them from seeing the truth in Christ. (2 Corinthians 4:3–4).

- Promise to research and return if you don't know the answer to a question.
- Remember a believer in Christ is not an expert or an attorney but a witness.
- Don't be discouraged; you are not expected to have all the answers.
- Most people will appreciate and understand if you honestly admit you cannot adequately answer their question.
- Write down the question, research the answer, and then return it to the person with the proper answer. Look it up. Ask a friend or pastor.

Two common objections are the following:

1. "I don't believe the Bible."

    Most of these objections are from people who believe they are too intellectual to believe the Bible. In other words, they feel they are too smart to believe in *just the Bible*. It is important that this type of person does not feel ignorant in front of us. You might say, "The main message of the Bible is how a person may have eternal life. What do you understand the Bible teaches about that?" 99% of the time, he/she will respond with what is called a *works answer*. An example of a "works answer" would be, "You must be good or keep the Ten Commandments." Then you can say, "That's what I was afraid of. You have rejected the Bible without

understanding its main message." Then share the gospel.
2. One of the ways we can know that the Bible is authentic and true is through fulfilled Old Testament prophecy. You may want to read prophecies one by one from the Old Testament, that point to Christ. You may want to have a list of the prophecies handy to refer to. Start with the clearest prophecies about Christ being born of a virgin, in Bethlehem, etc. As you read each prophecy, ask, "Who do you think the Bible is speaking about?" After they answer "Jesus" a few times, they will see the pattern and continue to reply "Jesus" for the rest of the Old Testament prophecies.

You might ask, "Can you explain that?" They will probably wonder what you mean. Explain that the prophecies you read were from the Old Testament, that they were written hundreds of years before they were fulfilled, and yet they were fulfilled in detail in Jesus's life. Just as they were prophesied. Then tell them there aren't just a few, but there are over 333 prophecies that were all fulfilled in Christ. The chances of all of those being fulfilled in one person are mind-boggling. The only explanation is that the Bible is a supernatural book, and the prophecies were revealed by the all-knowing God who knows the end from the beginning!

Christian apologetics is a term that means to be able to give a verbal defense for the gospel or Christianity. I believe we do this in many ways by being a living example of our faith, by sharing our story or testimony, and by sharing the gospel. Some people want scientific facts and deeper theology, and it is always good to be armed with this information for these people. There are many great books and resources on Christian apologetics. I would highly recommend you familiarize yourself with some of these. *However*, I have led thousands of people to put their faith in Jesus without them raising any questions. You don't have to wait until you feel you have all the answers to share your faith just always be learning all along the way.

This book is to equip you to understand the basis of the Christian faith for yourself and to be able to share and teach it. It will help you share with anyone who is seeking to know about the gospel of Jesus Christ and how to receive eternal life. You don't have to be an expert. Remember Jesus said, "Go. You will learn more as you go."

Review

Scripture:

> Sanctify the Lord God in your hearts, and be ready always to be able to give an answer to every man that asks you a reason for the hope that is in you with meekness and fear (respect). (1 Peter 3:15)

Practical application: Be kind when sharing the gospel even if people reject it or are rude.

CHANGE

Prayer: Father, give me the boldness and courage to share my faith. You promise at that moment that You will fill our mouths with the right words and give us the right attitude if we need it.

CHAPTER 14

Final Thoughts

There is no greater change in this world than personal change that comes from accepting Jesus Christ as your personal savior. It is miraculous. The second greatest change is knowing your God and understanding your faith—it is an anchor in your life. Lastly, there is no more life-changing and fulfilling joy than leading and teaching others to share their faith. This is my greatest desire in this life—to help others receive eternal life, to understand the good news of the gospel…and to help Christians learn how to teach others.

Your faith and love are action words. It is now time to get started. Take action now. This life is short. Begin praying for yourself and others. Be kind to others. Write your story and learn the gospel. Go and share it with others. It is the greatest act of love we have to give to others.

In closing, I would like to pray for you. You have been commissioned by Jesus to go into all the world and preach the gospel.

Let's pray.

Father God, I pray for each of those who have read this book and heard Your word. We acknowledge it was not by accident. Now empower them by Your Holy Spirit to go into all the world. Remind them that You are with them and will equip them in whatever You have called them to do. May they be a light wherever they go, and may signs and wonders follow them. In Jesus's name, amen.

Give a man fish, he eats for a day. Teach him to fish, he eats for a lifetime. Train him further, and he owns a whole chain of seafood restaurants.

You can contact us at Friendlyfaithsharing@gmail.com or Friendlyfaithsharing.com.

ACKNOWLEDGMENTS

Special thank-you to Kelly C. Moore Trent, Edi Smith Wohlgemuth, Wayne and Debra Ramsay, Barry and Beverly Chandler, Karen Foster, Pastor Steve McCoy, and to all the many other pastors, ministers, friends, and family. Thank you with all my heart.

ABOUT THE AUTHOR

Pastor Tina Trent was born and raised in Jacksonville, Florida. In 1988, she had a life-changing experience when she received eternal life and pursued the call of God on her life. Soon after, she went to work on staff at her church, where she served for over thirty years on the pastoral staff and as an executive pastor.

She has taught Bible in a Christian school for many years and has a passion for sharing the love of God and helping others learn about the gospel of Jesus Christ. She also served on the advisory board of a youth evangelism, international ministry, where she served for eighteen years.

Pastor Tina assisted in three revisions of the youth curriculum that have been taught around the world. Inspired by God, she wrote a Bible-based, easy-to-understand curriculum in 1996 on how to share your faith for adults and youth called Friendly Faith Sharing (FFS). Through the years, FFS has continued to develop and grow. She also wrote a specialized curriculum tailored for prison ministry and has taught thousands of prisoners at Lawtey Correctional Institution on how to effectively share their faith. She went on to develop and write *Kid's Friendly Faith Sharing* curriculum and has taught *Kids FFS* for many years, training up a future generation of leaders. *Kids FFS* is currently translated into two languages.

Pastor Tina has a passion for the local church and its missions. She has conducted pastor's training nationally and internationally as well as trained thousands of preschoolers, kids, youth, adults, pastors, and prisoners to effectively share their faith. She has trained and led adults and youth on many international mission trips to share and teach the gospel. Currently, she continues to lead and counsel others and consults and helps church leadership. Pastor Tina will continue to faithfully fulfill the great commission of Jesus that tells us to "go into all the world and share the good news" (Mark 16:15) and to "make disciples of all nations baptizing them in the name of the Father, and of the Son, and of the Holy Spirit" (Matthew 28:19).

Printed in the USA
CPSIA information can be obtained
at www.ICGtesting.com
LVHW090608150924
791034LV00001B/224